C000134620

Paths of the Spirit

Acknowledgements
Introduction and commentary by Harvey Gillman
Cover and layout design by Roger Holloway

Photographs by:
Andrew Backhouse
Robin Coutts
Harvey Gillman
Roger Holloway
Diana Roantree
The Imperial War Museum

First edition, published March 1998 by

Quaker Home Service
Friends House, Euston Road, London NW1 2BJ

© Britain Yearly Meeting 1998

All rights reserved. No part of this book may be
reproduced or utilised, in any form or by any
means, electronic or
mechanical, including photocopying, recording, or
by any
information or storage system without permission
in writing from the Publisher.

ISBN 0-85245-294-2

QHS
Quaker Home Service
'books to nurture the spirit'

Paths of the Spirit

A book of meditations in
words and pictures based
upon extracts from
Quaker faith and practice,
arranged by Harvey Gillman.

To the reader:

The idea for this book came to me at Charney Manor, the Quaker retreat and study centre in Oxfordshire. During one session at a study weekend, the participants chose to read their favourite passages from *Quaker faith & practice*, an anthology of Quaker literature written during the three hundred and fifty years of the existence of the Religious Society of Friends. *Faith & practice*, revised once every generation or so, is a main source of inspiration and guidance for Quakers today. The passages were read in an exercise Quakers call worship sharing. We began in silence, a passage was read, and then silence ensued. People in the room had time to reflect on the words which they had just heard. It was a deep and moving experience.

Later I decided to put together a book of passages from *Faith & practice* as a book of meditations. In *Faith & practice*, which I consider to be a contemporary masterpiece, there are many passages of deep wisdom. The anthology you have here is only a brief sample of the contents but, I hope that these passages and the accompanying photographs may through their particular format lead you to experience something of the depth that we felt at the Charney gathering. The passages have been arranged and some introductory paragraphs and photographs have been added to give an atmosphere of the spiritual journey.

Spirituality is a web of relationships: our relationship with ourselves, with our families, our friends, our neighbours, with strangers, with animals, and with the environment in which we live and move – all held in the embrace of the Spirit. The spiritual path is about how we weave this web and how we deepen these connections throughout our lives.

The Quaker understanding is that there is a divine light in all people. This is our lantern on the way. Our worship is the attention we give to the light, our waiting upon it. In our daily lives we try, however haltingly, to shed this light upon the dark places. On the path we experience light and dark, we walk and we stumble. But we are not alone and as we progress there are visions of the divine commonwealth we can share with others.

To reflect this journey of the Spirit, I have divided this anthology into several sections: Love and Light, ... and Darkness, Worship, The Adventure of the World Around, Loneliness and Friendship, Visions of the Divine Commonwealth, and Wisdom and Serenity. I am aware that the paths we take are not always linear; darkness may reappear; and after moments of serenity, we may return to worry and confusion. Use the book as seems best to you.

One suggestion I would offer is for you to take each passage and each photograph of this book slowly, reflecting on what it says about your own life. If possible read the book in a silent place, read out of the silence and into the silence. Later you may wish to jot down the thoughts which come into your head as a result of the reading. Some of the passages may, as Quakers say, speak to your condition; others may not. However you are feeling, I hope you will find this book has something to say to you.

Harvey Gillman – August 97

Love and Light

We are on a spiritual path simply by being born; what helps us is the realisation that there is something within that can guide us on this path.

Take heed, dear Friends, to the promptings of love and truth in your hearts. Trust them as the leadings of God whose light shows us our darkness and brings us to new life.

Advices and Queries

Ystyriwch, Gyfeillion annwyl, gymhellion cariad a gwirionedd yn eich calonnau.Ymddiriedwch ynddynt fel arweiniad Duw, Goleuni yr hwn sy'n dangos i ni ein tywyllwch gan ein dwyn i fywyd newydd.

Cynghorion a Holiadau

You will say, Christ saith this, and the apostles say this,
but what canst thou say? Art thou a child of Light and
hast walked in the Light, and what thou speakest is it
inwardly from God?

Margaret Fox quoting George Fox

I do believe that there is a power which is divine, creative and loving,
though we can often only describe it with the images and symbols that
rise from our particular experiences and those of our communities. This
power is part and parcel of all things, human, animal, indeed of all that
lives. Its story is greater than any one cultural version of it and yet it is
embodied in all stories, in all traditions. It is a power that paradoxically
needs the human response. Like us it is energised by the reciprocity of
love.

It wills us our redemption, longs for us to turn to it. It does not create
heaven and hell for us, but allows us to do that for ourselves. Such is the
terrible vulnerability of love.

Harvey Gillman

In every homeless child, every refugee, every criminal or outcast, every worker or preacher, those in authority and those without it, there is a child of God, one who is precious and loved.

Janet Scott

The light for which the world longs is already shining. It is shining into the darkness, but the darkness does not apprehend it. It is shining into the darkness, but the darkness is not overcoming it. It is shining in many a soul, and already the new order has begun within the kingdom of the heart. It is shining in many a small group and creating a heavenly-earthly fellowship of children of the light. It will always shine and lead many into the world of need, that they may bear it up into the heart of God.

Thomas R Kelly

Love is the hardest lesson in Christianity; but, for that reason, it should be most our care to learn it.

William Penn

What is my religion? My friends, my teachers, my God. And who is my God? He speaks within me: if I mishear, my friends correct me; if I misdo, I look to Jesus Christ. How then am I taught? I hear in the silence, I ponder in solitude, and I try in the noisy crowd to practise it. What do I learn? To put gaiety before prudence, grace before pleasure, service before power. What am I commanded? To seek patience in suffering, humility in success, steadfastness always. What is forbidden me? To reject another's love, to despise another's wisdom, to blaspheme another's God. And to what purpose? To help others so that we may enter the Commonwealth of Heaven together, each to find our Being in the Whole.

Frederick Parker Rhodes

What is Love? What shall I say of it, or how shall I in words express its nature? It is the sweetness of life; it is the sweet, tender, melting nature of God, flowing up through his seed of life into the creature, and of all things making the creature most like unto himself, both in nature and operation.

Isaac Penington

... and Darkness

On the path we may be overcome by darkness, whether it is a sense of the darkness within the self, or a sense of isolation and purposelessness in the world around. It may be a passing mist or a lasting fog and in this darkness all consolation may seem futile. We may experience a sense of being stuck as if there were no paths out of what Dante called the dark wood. But it is our trust that somewhere, even in the thickest confusion, there is a light.

The experience of many of the greatest saints points to the traversing of a dark night of the soul before the light of full communion dawns, and to times of dryness of spirit coming at intervals to test the faith and perseverance of the seeker.

T Edmund Harvey

I was under great temptations sometimes, and my inward
sufferings were heavy; but I could find none to open my condition
to but the Lord alone, unto whom I cried night and day.

George Fox

There are times when God and my personal faith seem to
be completely beyond my reach or understanding. These
are frightening times, because the work or activities I seek
to do have no apparent value or reason.

Bernard Brett

Art thou in the Darkness? Mind it not, for if thou dost it
will fill thee more, but stand still and act not, and wait in
patience till Light arises out of Darkness to lead thee. Art
thou wounded in conscience? Feed not there, but abide in
the Light which leads to Grace and Truth, which teaches
to deny, and puts off the weight, and removes the cause,
and brings saving health to Light.

James Nayler

Release

I was terrified I'd break down.
I did.
It didn't matter.
Rosalind M Baker

Sing and rejoice,
ye Children of the Day
and of the Light;
for the Lord is at work
in this thick night of Darkness
that may be felt:
and Truth doth flourish
as the rose,
and the lilies do grow
among the thorns,
and the plants atop of the hills,
and upon them the lambs
doth skip and play.
George Fox

I came back again and again in my own mind to this word Truth. 'Promptings of love and truth' – these two sometimes seem to be in conflict, but in fact they are inseparable. If we are to know the truth, we must be able to see with unclouded eyes, and then we will love what is real and not what is duty or fancy.

Alison Sharman

It is by encounter with our own darkness that we recognise the light. It is the light itself which shows us the darkness – and both are summoned within us.

Lorna M Marsden

Worship

Worship is the time given over to the divine within – and to the world around. It might be a time of rest, of inability to move forward, of powerlessness, or of joy; it might be a time of deep attentiveness on the journey itself, an inward and an outer journey.

Give over thine own willing, give over thy own running, give over thine own desiring to know or be anything and sink down to the seed which God sows in the heart, and let that grow in thee and be in thee and breathe in thee and act in thee; and thou shalt find by sweet experience that the Lord knows that and loves and owns that, and will lead it to the inheritance of Life, which is its portion.

Isaac Penington

As we learn more about worship we learn
to listen more deeply so that we can be
channels through which God's love
reaches the other person. It is God at
work, not we ourselves; we are simply
used.

Diana Lampen

Drop thy still dews of quietness,
Till all our strivings cease;
Take from our souls the strain and stress,
And let our ordered lives confess
The beauty of thy peace.

John Greenleaf Whittier

Silence itself ... has no magic. It may be just sheer emptiness, absence of words or noise or music. It may be an occasion for slumber, or it may be a dead form. But it may be an intensified pause, a vitalised hush, a creative quiet, an actual moment of mutual and reciprocal correspondence with God.

Rufus Jones

Here is no discipline in absent-mindedness. Walk and talk and work and laugh with your friends. But behind the scenes keep up the life of simple prayer and inward worship. Keep it up throughout the day. Let inward prayer be your last act before you fall asleep and the first act when you awake. And in time you will find, as did Brother Lawrence, that 'those who have the gale of the Holy Spirit go forward even in sleep'.

Thomas R Kelly

Prayer alone can reopen the road to the Spirit, blocked repeatedly by busyness, self-importance, self-indulgence, self-pity, depression or despair.

Donald Court

True worship may be experienced at any time; in any place – alone on the hills or in the busy daily life – we may find God, in whom we live and move and have our being. But this individual experience is not sufficient, and in a meeting held in the Spirit there is a giving and receiving between its members, one helping another with or without words. So there may come a wider vision and a deeper experience.

The 1925 and 1994 Revision Committees

As I silence myself I become more sensitive to the sounds around me, and I do not block them out. The songs of birds, the rustle of the wind, children in the playground, the roar of an airplane overhead are all taken into my worship ... I think of myself like the tree planted by the 'rivers of water' in Psalm 1, sucking up God's gift of life and being restored.

Tayeko Yamanouchi

The people whom I know who live a truly nonviolent life are in touch with the source of power, call it what you will; the Light, the seed, God, the holy spirit. Many others of us find this wellspring when we need it, and lose it again, find it and lose it, find it and lose it.

Jo Vellacott

There is the healing that comes through prayer
in its various forms, through the laying on of
hands, through music and dance, painting and
colour, through communication with and
understanding of the world of nature, and
through friendship.

Jim Pym

All our senses are given to us to enjoy, and to praise God.
The smell of the sea, of the blossom borne on the wind, of
the soft flesh of a little baby; the taste of a ripe plum or
bread fresh from the oven, the feel of warm cat's fur, or
the body of a lover – these are all forms of thanksgiving
prayer.

Bella Bown

The Adventure of the World Around

Having found the lantern or at least being guided by its reflections, and having become aware of the marvels and the challenges of the world both within and outside, we can then move out in boldness.

I should like to change the name 'seekers' to 'explorers'.
There is a considerable difference there: we do not seek
the Atlantic, we explore it.

Ole Olden

It is 'life' only that can lead to life, and no forms are availing without it.
Seek the life in all things, and cherish it by all authorised means.

Hannah Kilham

A sudden concentration of attention on a rainy August morning. Clusters of bright red berries, some wrinkled, some blemished, others perfect, hanging among green leaves. The experience could not have lasted more than a few seconds, but that was a moment out of time. I was caught up in what I saw: I became a part of it: the berries, the leaves, the raindrops and I, we were all of a piece. A moment of beauty and harmony and meaning. A moment of understanding.

Ralph Hetherington

The exploration of the minute
structure of matter seems to take us as
far into the unknown as does the
exploration of the farthest reaches of
space.

Howard H Brinton

I was early convinced in my mind that true religion consisted in an inward life wherein the heart doth love and reverence God in the Creator and learns to exercise true justice and goodness not only toward all men but also toward the brute creation; that as the mind was moved on an inward principle to love God as an invisible, incomprehensible being, on the same principle, it was moved to love him in all his manifestations in the visible world; that as by his breath the flame of life was kindled in all animal and sensitive creatures, to say we love God ... and at the same time exercise cruelty toward the least creature ... was a contradiction in itself.

John Woolman

Along the path of the imagination the artist and mystic make contact. The revelations of God are not all of one kind. Always the search in art, as in religion, is for the rhythms of relationships, for the unity, the urge, the mystery, the wonder of life that is presented in great art and true religion.

Horace B Pointing

We live on the wave's edge, where sea, sand and sky
are all mixed up together: we are tossed head over
heels in the surf, catching only occasional glimpses of
any fixed horizon. Some of us stay there from choice
because it is exciting and it *feels like the right place to be.*
Philip Rack

Creativity is the gift that we were given on the eighth day of creation. In naming and re-making the world we are co-workers with God, and whether we are making a garden or a meal, a painting or a piece of furniture or a computer program, we are sharing in an ongoing act of creation through which the world is constantly re-made.

Jo Farrow

This is a marvellous world, full of beauty and splendour; it is also an unrelenting and savage world, and we are not the only living things prone to dominate if given the chance. In our fumbling, chaotic way, we do also make gardens, irrigate the desert, fly to the moon and compose symphonies. Some of us are trying to save species other than ourselves.

We have no reason to be either arrogant or complacent: one look at the stars or through a microscope is sufficient to quell such notions. But we have to accept our position in the world with as much grace, responsibility and fortitude as we can muster, and try to grow up to our mission of love in this tangle of prospects and torments.

Pamela Umbima

Loneliness and Friendship

There are times when we do not feel connected. The path is a wide one on which there are many companions, but there are times when it feels very narrow and we sense our isolation. There may be at this point a temptation to rush into a false sense of community to hide from the true self. True community is based on a sense of the value of each person, when the integrity of each is respected.

The Kingdom of Heaven did gather us and catch us all, as in a net, and his heavenly power at one time drew many hundreds to land. We came to know a place to stand in and what to wait in...

Francis Howgill

Where there is genuine tenderness, an openness to responsibility, and the seed of commitment, God is surely not shut out. Can we not say that God can enter any relationship in which there is a measure of selfless love? – and is not every generalisation we make qualified by this?

Towards a Quaker view of sex

It was said of early Christians, ' Behold, how they love one another'. Could this equally be said for us?

June Ellis

Friends are not about building walls but about taking
them down.

Some members of North Northumberland Meeting

To be human is to be a separate person, and therefore, to know the fact and
the mystery of aloneness. Although I find I can make surface contact with
people quite readily, I am often lonely and experience stretches of doubt
and dryness. Then especially I need friends who will accept a quality of
friendship which involves praying for me. By this I mean that they care
enough to think of me, to ask themselves if there is any special need of
mine they can meet, to commend what they don't know about me to God's
wisdom, and when we meet to make me welcome.

Donald Court

Busy lovers find time to write letters to one another,
often ... long letters; although what really matters is
not the length of the letter any more than it is the
length of the prayer. In this life we find the time for
what we believe to be important.

Douglas Steere

What is the ground and foundation of the gathered
meeting? In the last analysis, it is, I am convinced, the
Real Presence of God.

Thomas R Kelly

*But community grows from within. It does not imply uniformity . Margaret Fox
had to warn early Friends against imposing uniformity of dress as an outward
form.*

We are now coming into that which Christ cried woe against, minding
altogether outward things, neglecting the inward work of Almighty God in
our hearts ... in so much that poor Friends is mangled in their minds, that
they know not what to do, for one Friend says one way, and another, but
Christ Jesus saith, that we must take no thought what we shall eat, or what
we shall drink, or what we shall put on, but bids us consider the lilies how
they grow, in more royalty than Solomon ... It is more fit for us, to be
covered with God's Eternal Spirit, and clothed with his Eternal Light,
which leads us and guides us into righteousness.

Margaret Fox

... we are individuals and ... we are alone but, as part of a loving community, to be alone does not necessarily mean to be lonely.

Epistle of Junior Yearly Meeting

Our lives have recently been transformed by the birth of a baby daughter. Nothing we read or were told could prepare us for the total revolution in our lives which the arrival of this beautiful spirit into our midst has brought. I feel that I am living on a new plane since the muffled kicks and hiccups of pregnancy were revealed to be a perfect and wonderful human being...

That moment of timelessness and joy was like a glimpse of heaven, seen through the miracle of birth with the endless possibilities for discovery, growth and love for all three of us.

Peter Wallis

Our children are given to us for a
time to cherish, to protect, to
nurture, and then to salute as
they go their separate ways.
Elizabeth Watson

Do we have enough confidence in each other to know that our problems as well as our convictions and uncertainties can be shared with understanding? How is the child and the stranger received among us? Do we see our young people as individuals we want to know and care for and do we want to provide opportunities when they can get to know and care for us?

Peggy McGeoghegan

The loneliness which we rightly dread is not the absence of human faces and voices – it is the absence of love ... Our wisdom therefore must lie in learning not to shrink from anything that may be in store for us, but so to grasp the master key of life as to be able to turn everything to good and fruitful account.

Caroline E Stephen

In the journey through life, as we grow and mature, live singly or in a relationship with others our sexuality will grow, develop and change. Our sexual needs, drives and fantasies will be different at different stages in our life – as a teenager, a partner, a parent, an older person. Our sexuality is, throughout, an expression of ourselves. It is an integral part of our humanity and as such is subject to the leadings of the spirit. We should therefore give thanks for our sexuality and seek to nurture it both within ourselves and in our loving relationships.

Bill Edgar

Visions of the Divine Commonwealth

At any moment, even amid great darkness, a vision may appear, a vision of how things and we ourselves may be different. We may become aware of another way of being. We may better understand our place in the sacred web – our place as individuals and as communities, where the spiritual, the social and the political are joined together.

There is a spirit which I feel that delights to do no evil, nor to revenge any wrong, but delights to endure all things, in hope to enjoy its own in the end. Its hope is to outlive all wrath and contention, and to weary out all exaltation and cruelty, or whatever is of a nature contrary to itself. It sees to the end of all temptations. As it bears no evil in itself, so it conceives none in thoughts to any other. If it be betrayed, it bears it, for its ground and spring is the mercies and forgiveness of God. Its crown is meekness, its life is everlasting love unfeigned; it takes its kingdom with entreaty and not with contention, and keeps it by lowliness of mind. In God alone it can rejoice, though none else regard it, or can own its life. It's conceived in sorrow, and brought forth without any to pity it, nor doth it murmur at grief and oppression. It never rejoiceth but through sufferings; for with the world's joy it is murdered. I found it alone, being forsaken. I have fellowship therein with them who lived in dens and desolate places in the earth, who through death obtained this resurrection and eternal holy life.

James Nayler

I ask for daily bread, but not for wealth,
lest I forget the poor.
I ask for strength, but not for power,
lest I despise the meek.
I ask for wisdom, but not for learning,
lest I scorn the simple.
I ask for a clean name, but not for fame,
lest I contemn the lowly.
I ask for peace of mind, but not for idle hours,
lest I fail to hearken to the call of duty.

Inazo Nitobe

Out of the depths of authentic prayer comes a
longing for peace and a passion for justice.

Gordon Matthews

What shall I say? I have met with the true peace, the true
righteousness, the true holiness, the true rest of the soul, the
everlasting habitation which the redeemed dwell in.

Isaac Penington

I told [the Commonwealth Commissioners] I lived in the
virtue of that life and power that took away the occasion of
all wars ... I told them I was come into the covenant of peace
which was before wars and strife were.

George Fox

Do you, as disciples of Christ, take a living
interest in the social conditions of the district
in which you live?

Advices and Queries

As Friends, we cannot separate our religious calling from our practical work for the kingdom of God.

Quaker Home Service conference on wardenship

Compassion to be effective requires
detailed knowledge andunderstanding of
how society works.

Grigor McClelland

The political and social struggles must be waged, but a person is more and needs more than politics, else we are in danger of gaining the whole world but losing our souls.

Eva I Pinthus

God was in Christ, reconciling the world
to himself, and he calls each of us to a
ministry or vocation of reconciliation.

Sydney Bailey

The weapons of the Spirit: love, truth-saying,
nonviolence, the good news of God's birth and rebirth
among us, imagination, vision, and laughter.

Mary Lou Leavitt

We are a people that follow after those things that make for peace, love
and unity; it is our desire that others' feet may walk in the same, and do
deny and bear our testimony against all strife, and wars, and
contentions that come from the lusts that war in the members, that war
in the soul, which we wait for, and watch for in all people, and love and
desire the good of all... Treason, treachery, and false dealing we do
utterly deny; false dealing, surmising, or plotting against any creature
upon the face of the earth, and speak the truth in plainness, and
singleness of heart.

Paper from Margaret Fell to Charles II

Wisdom and Serenity

Remember that each one of us is
unique, precious, a child of God.
Advices and Queries

Cofiwch fod pob un ohonom yn unigryw,
yn werthfawr, yn blentyn i Dduw.
Cynghorion a holiadau

Are there not different states, different degrees, different growths, different places? ... Therefore, watch every one to feel and know his own places and service in the body, and to be sensible of the gifts, places, and services of others, that the Lord may be honoured in all, and every one owned and honoured in the Lord...

Isaac Penington

We none of us are members because we have attained a certain standard of goodness, but rather because, in this matter, we still are all humble learners in the school of Christ.

Edgar Dunstan

We must be confident that there is still more 'life' to be 'lived' and yet more heights to be scaled. The tragedy of middle age is that, so often, men and women cease to press 'towards the goal of their high calling'. They cease learning, cease growing; they give up and resign from life. As wisdom dawns with age, we begin to measure our experiences not by what life gives to us, not by the things withheld from us, but by their power to help us to grow in spiritual wisdom.

Evelyn Sturge

I am convinced it is a great art to know how to grow old gracefully, and I am determined to practise it... I always thought I should love to grow old, and I find it even more delightful than I thought. It is so delicious to be *done* with things, and to feel no need any longer to content myself much about earthly affairs ... I am tremendously content to let one activity after another go, and to await quietly and happily the opening of the door at the end of the passage-way, that will let me in to my real abiding place.

Hannah Whitall Smith

Death is but crossing the world, as
friends do the seas; they live in one
another still.

William Penn

Part of understanding life and one's place
in life is to form a 'right' relationship
with things ... to seek mastery is not to
gain a 'right' relationship.

Jim Platts

I am glad I was here. Now I am clear, I am fully clear ... All is well; the Seed of God reigns over all and over death itself. And though I am weak in body, yet the power of God is over all, and the Seed reigns over all disorderly spirits.

George Fox

Now I was come up in spirit through the flaming sword into the paradise of God. All things were new, and all the creation gave another smell unto me than before, beyond what words can utter.

George Fox

To face up to the fact of death gives a
fuller awareness of God-given life.

Jenifer Faulkner

Love bridges death.

John Wilhelm Rowntree

Harvey Gillman is Outreach Secretary of Quaker Home Service. He has been a Quaker since 1978. He trained as a teacher in French and Italian and has spoken on topics related to the Quaker movement throughout Great Britain, in New Zealand, Germany, Italy, in Cuba and the United States. He has written amongst other publications: *A Minority of One*, which is his spiritual autobiography; *A Light that is Shining*, an introduction to Quakers; *Spiritual Hospitality*, a Quaker's view on outreach; and *New Models, New Relationships*, a lecture given to German Quakers based on faith and practice in the light of our images of God. He is at present co-leading an ecumenical course in spiritual direction – although he does not find the latter term satisfactory. He also writes poetry and is a passionate patio gardener, and lives with his partner and three cats in Sussex.

NOTES

Numbers refer to paragraphs of *Quaker Faith & Practice*. This book is available from the Quaker Bookshop, Friends House, Euston Road, London, NW1 2BJ, tel: 0171-663 1030/1. Standard paperback £6.50; large print paperback £7.50; standard cloth £11.00; large print cloth £10.00. Dates refer to the year in which the reference was written or spoken unless otherwise stated. References from George Fox's *Journal* come from the Nickalls edition of 1952 unless otherwise stated.

LIGHT AND LOVE

1.021 *Advices and Queries* forms the first paragraph of *Quaker faith & practice*, 1995 (English and Welsh).
19.07 Margaret Fox, quoted in George Fox's *Journal*, 1694
26.31 Harvey Gillman, *A minority of one*, 1988
26.50 Janet Scott, *What canst thou say?*, 1980
26.62 Thomas R Kelly, *Wider Quaker Fellowship annual report*, 1941
22.01 William Penn, *'Some Fruits of Solitude'*, 1693
26.41 Frederick Parker-Rhodes, *The Friend*, 1977
26.30 Isaac Penington, *Some of the mysteries of God's kingdom glanced at*, 1663

... AND DARKNESS

2.31 T Edmund Harvey, *Along the road of prayer*, 1929
19.03 George Fox, *Journal*, 1647
21.61 Bernard Brett, *A passing traveller: the life of Bernard Brett in his own words*, 1987
21.65 James Nayler, *A collection of sundry books, epistles and papers*, circa 1659
21.67 Rosalind M Baker, *The Friend*, 1986
20.23 George Fox, *letter*, 1663
20.75 Alison Sharman, *The Friend*, 1986
21.10 Lorna M Marsden, *The Friend*, 1983

WORSHIP

26.70 Isaac Penington, *Some directions to the panting soul*, 1671
2.26 Diana Lampen, *Facing death*, 1979
20.03 John Greenleaf Whittier, *The Brewing of Soma* 1872

2.16 Rufus Jones, 'The spiritual message of the Religious Society of Friends', *in Friends World Conference, Report of Commission*, 1937

2.22 Thomas R Kelly, A *testament of devotion*, 1941

20.09 Donald Court, *Leading a double life*, 1970

2.11 Drafted by 1925 and amended by 1994 Revision Committee

2.54 Tayeko Yamanouchi, Ways *of worship*, 1980

20.05 Jo Vellacott, *Women, Peace and Power*, 1982

21.72 Jim Pym, *What kind of God, what kind of healing?*, 1990

21.24 Bella Bown, written about 1980

THE ADVENTURE OF THE WORLD AROUND

26.17 Ole Olden, *The Friend*, 1955

21.26 Memoir of the late Hannah Kilham, ed Sarah Biller, 1837

20.06 Philip Rack, *The Friend*, 1979

21.42 Howard H Brinton, *Creative worship*, 1931

25.05 John Woolman, *Journal*, 1772

21.32 Horace B Pointing, *Art, religion and the common life*, 1944

21.27 Ralph Hetherington, *The sense of glory: a psychological study of peak-experiences*, 1975

21.38 Jo Farrow, 1994

25.08 Pamela Umbima, *The Friend*, 1992

LONELINESS AND FRIENDSHIP

19.08 'Francis Howgill's testimony concerning ... Edward Burrough', 1663

22.18 Group of Friends, *Towards a Quaker view of sex*, 1963

10.11 June Ellis, *Quaker Social Responsibility & Education journal*, 1986

10.31 Text by some members of North Northumberland Meeting submitted to Yearly Meeting, 1994

10.33 Donald Court, A *scientific age and a declining church: what has a Friend to say?*, 1965

2.32 Douglas Steere, *Prayer and worship*, 1938

2.40 Thomas R Kelly, *The gathered meeting*, 1940

20.31 Margaret Fell, manuscript Portfolio 56/66 in the Library of the Society of Friends. The passage is considerably abridged and omissions are not indicated in the text, circa 1700. The dots in this extract refer to omissions

VISIONS OF THE DIVINE COMMONWEALTH

WISDOM AND SERENITY

Further Reading

A Light that is Shining - an introduction to Quakers - HARVEY GILLMAN
A clear and engaging introduction to Friends. It tells of their religious convictions, form of worship and their political and social insights.
QHS, 1997

Yours in Friendship - RICHARD ALLEN
In a series of letters the author introduces Quakerism to a new attender - but even Quakers of many years standing will find it explain things they didn't realise they didn't know.
QHS, 1995

Amazing Fact of Quaker Worship - GEORGE GORMAN
Written with sustained dignity and conviction, speaking from a life deeply centred in the silence of Quaker worship.
QHS, 1973

Encounter with Silence - reflections from the Quaker tradition - JOHN PUNSHON
FUP & QHS, 1987

Quaker Faith & Practice
The book of Christian discipline of the Yearly Meeting of the religious Society of Friends (Quakers) in Britain.
QHS, 1995

Obtainable from the Quaker Bookshop, Friends House, 173-177 Euston Road, London NW1 2BJ.
Tel 0171 663 1030